Inventory Expenses From Non-Traditional Sources

This material has been prepared for informational purposes only, and is not intended to provide, and should not be relied on for, tax, legal or accounting advice. You should consult your own tax, legal and accounting advisors.

Copyright ©2019 Truly Found LLC

ISBN: 978-109624-195-9

Printed in the United States of America

First printing edition 2019.

For product inquiries, contact: trulyfound@outlook.com

Owner's Information

Name _____

Business _____

Dates covered
      From _____
      To   _____

Email _____

Cell number _____

Address _____
_____
_____

Overview & Examples

Use this journal for recording expenses of inventory purchases made from non-standard sources, such as garage or yard sales, auctions, estate sales, antique malls, or flea markets. Most of the time, you will not have a receipt from these places and it is important to document expenses for tax and business accounting purposes. When you are on the road, it can be tough to enter the data into your mobile smartphone or tablet. So, use this handy journal to track your expenses in real-time. Then, you can enter the data into your computer when you have the time and check off the appropriate box in the journal entry.

The next page shows the layout of the journal along with two completed examples. The example at the top of the page shows purchases at one yard sale. The second example shows how you could document purchases for a community yard sale. You can experiment with your own creative ways to get the most out of this journal. Happy Treasure Hunting!

Inventory Expenses

Date	Cost ($)	Miles Driven
4-28-19	$75.00	19 mi

Location: Yard sale - Athens GA

Entered into PC: [ ]

Items Purchased
- 3 watches
- Model trains
- Vintage cookbooks
- Box of DVDs

EXAMPLES

Date	Cost ($)	Miles Driven
5-4-19	$317.00	47 mi

Location: Community Yard Sales in Mesa AZ

Entered into PC: [X]

Items Purchased
- 1 - Box of old magazines — $10
- 2 - Wood night stand — $8
- 2 - Vintage telephone — $2
- 3 - Box of old tools — $12
- 4 - Assorted jewelry — $35
- 5 - Coin collection — $250

Inventory Expenses

Date	Cost ($)	Miles Driven

Location _____   Entered into PC ☐

Items Purchased

_____
_____
_____
_____
_____
_____
_____

Date	Cost ($)	Miles Driven

Location _____   Entered into PC ☐

Items Purchased

_____
_____
_____
_____
_____
_____
_____

Inventory Expenses

Date	Cost ($)	Miles Driven

Location
_____

Entered into PC ☐

Items Purchased

_____
_____
_____
_____
_____
_____
_____
_____

Date	Cost ($)	Miles Driven

Location
_____

Entered into PC ☐

Items Purchased

_____
_____
_____
_____
_____
_____
_____
_____

Inventory Expenses

Date	Cost ($)	Miles Driven

Location
_____

Entered into PC [ ]

Items Purchased

_____
_____
_____
_____
_____
_____
_____

Date	Cost ($)	Miles Driven

Location
_____

Entered into PC [ ]

Items Purchased

_____
_____
_____
_____
_____
_____
_____

Inventory Expenses

Date	Cost ($)	Miles Driven

Location _____

Entered into PC [ ]

Items Purchased

_____
_____
_____
_____
_____
_____
_____

Date	Cost ($)	Miles Driven

Location _____

Entered into PC [ ]

Items Purchased

_____
_____
_____
_____
_____
_____
_____

Inventory Expenses

Date	Cost ($)	Miles Driven

Location
_____

Items Purchased
_____
_____
_____
_____
_____
_____

Entered into PC ☐

Date	Cost ($)	Miles Driven

Location
_____

Items Purchased
_____
_____
_____
_____
_____
_____

Entered into PC ☐

Inventory Expenses

Date	Cost ($)	Miles Driven

Location
_____

Entered into PC [ ]

Items Purchased

_____
_____
_____
_____
_____
_____
_____
_____

Date	Cost ($)	Miles Driven

Location
_____

Entered into PC [ ]

Items Purchased

_____
_____
_____
_____
_____
_____
_____
_____

Inventory Expenses

Date	Cost ($)	Miles Driven

Location
_____

Entered into PC [ ]

Items Purchased

_____
_____
_____
_____
_____
_____
_____

Date	Cost ($)	Miles Driven

Location
_____

Entered into PC [ ]

Items Purchased

_____
_____
_____
_____
_____
_____
_____

Inventory Expenses

Date	Cost ($)	Miles Driven

Location _____

Entered into PC [ ]

Items Purchased

_____
_____
_____
_____
_____
_____
_____
_____

Date	Cost ($)	Miles Driven

Location _____

Entered into PC [ ]

Items Purchased

_____
_____
_____
_____
_____
_____
_____
_____

Inventory Expenses

Date	Cost ($)	Miles Driven

Location
_____

Items Purchased

_____
_____
_____
_____
_____
_____
_____

Entered into PC ☐

Date	Cost ($)	Miles Driven

Location
_____

Items Purchased

_____
_____
_____
_____
_____
_____
_____

Entered into PC ☐

Inventory Expenses

Date	Cost ($)	Miles Driven

Location _____

Entered into PC [ ]

Items Purchased

_____
_____
_____
_____
_____
_____
_____
_____

Date	Cost ($)	Miles Driven

Location _____

Entered into PC [ ]

Items Purchased

_____
_____
_____
_____
_____
_____
_____
_____

Inventory Expenses

Date	Cost ($)	Miles Driven

Location _____ Entered into PC ☐

Items Purchased

_____
_____
_____
_____
_____
_____
_____

Date	Cost ($)	Miles Driven

Location _____ Entered into PC ☐

Items Purchased

_____
_____
_____
_____
_____
_____
_____

Inventory Expenses

Date	Cost ($)	Miles Driven

Location
_____

Items Purchased
_____
_____
_____
_____
_____
_____
_____

Entered into PC [ ]

Date	Cost ($)	Miles Driven

Location
_____

Items Purchased
_____
_____
_____
_____
_____
_____
_____

Entered into PC [ ]

Inventory Expenses

Date	Cost ($)	Miles Driven

Location
_____

Items Purchased

Entered into PC [ ]

_____
_____
_____
_____
_____
_____
_____

Date	Cost ($)	Miles Driven

Location
_____

Items Purchased

Entered into PC [ ]

_____
_____
_____
_____
_____
_____
_____

Inventory Expenses

Date	Cost ($)	Miles Driven

Location
_____

Entered into PC ☐

Items Purchased
_____
_____
_____
_____
_____
_____
_____
_____

Date	Cost ($)	Miles Driven

Location
_____

Entered into PC ☐

Items Purchased
_____
_____
_____
_____
_____
_____
_____
_____

Inventory Expenses

Date	Cost ($)	Miles Driven

Location
_____

Items Purchased

_____
_____
_____
_____
_____
_____

Entered into PC ☐

Date	Cost ($)	Miles Driven

Location
_____

Items Purchased

_____
_____
_____
_____
_____
_____

Entered into PC ☐

Inventory Expenses

Date	Cost ($)	Miles Driven

Location _____

Entered into PC [ ]

Items Purchased

_____
_____
_____
_____
_____
_____
_____

Date	Cost ($)	Miles Driven

Location _____

Entered into PC [ ]

Items Purchased

_____
_____
_____
_____
_____
_____
_____

Inventory Expenses

Date	Cost ($)	Miles Driven

Location _____

Entered into PC [ ]

Items Purchased

_____
_____
_____
_____
_____
_____
_____

Date	Cost ($)	Miles Driven

Location _____

Entered into PC [ ]

Items Purchased

_____
_____
_____
_____
_____
_____
_____

Inventory Expenses

Date	Cost ($)	Miles Driven

Location _____

Entered into PC ☐

Items Purchased

_____
_____
_____
_____
_____
_____
_____

Date	Cost ($)	Miles Driven

Location _____

Entered into PC ☐

Items Purchased

_____
_____
_____
_____
_____
_____
_____

Inventory Expenses

Date	Cost ($)	Miles Driven

Location
_____

Entered into PC ☐

Items Purchased
_____
_____
_____
_____
_____
_____
_____

Date	Cost ($)	Miles Driven

Location
_____

Entered into PC ☐

Items Purchased
_____
_____
_____
_____
_____
_____
_____

Inventory Expenses

Date	Cost ($)	Miles Driven

Location
_____

Entered into PC [   ]

Items Purchased
_____
_____
_____
_____
_____
_____
_____
_____

Date	Cost ($)	Miles Driven

Location
_____

Entered into PC [   ]

Items Purchased
_____
_____
_____
_____
_____
_____
_____
_____

Inventory Expenses

Date	Cost ($)	Miles Driven

Location
_____

Entered into PC [ ]

Items Purchased
_____
_____
_____
_____
_____
_____
_____

Date	Cost ($)	Miles Driven

Location
_____

Entered into PC [ ]

Items Purchased
_____
_____
_____
_____
_____
_____
_____

Inventory Expenses

Date	Cost ($)	Miles Driven

Location
_____

Entered into PC [ ]

Items Purchased
_____
_____
_____
_____
_____
_____
_____

Date	Cost ($)	Miles Driven

Location
_____

Entered into PC [ ]

Items Purchased
_____
_____
_____
_____
_____
_____
_____

Inventory Expenses

Date	Cost ($)	Miles Driven

Location
_____

Entered into PC [ ]

Items Purchased

_____
_____
_____
_____
_____
_____
_____

Date	Cost ($)	Miles Driven

Location
_____

Entered into PC [ ]

Items Purchased

_____
_____
_____
_____
_____
_____
_____

Inventory Expenses

Date	Cost ($)	Miles Driven

Location _____ Entered into PC ☐

Items Purchased

_____
_____
_____
_____
_____
_____
_____

Date	Cost ($)	Miles Driven

Location _____ Entered into PC ☐

Items Purchased

_____
_____
_____
_____
_____
_____
_____

Inventory Expenses

Date	Cost ($)	Miles Driven

Location
_____

Entered into PC [ ]

Items Purchased
_____
_____
_____
_____
_____
_____
_____

Date	Cost ($)	Miles Driven

Location
_____

Entered into PC [ ]

Items Purchased
_____
_____
_____
_____
_____
_____
_____

Inventory Expenses

Date	Cost ($)	Miles Driven

Location
_____

Entered into PC ☐

Items Purchased
_____
_____
_____
_____
_____
_____
_____
_____

Date	Cost ($)	Miles Driven

Location
_____

Entered into PC ☐

Items Purchased
_____
_____
_____
_____
_____
_____
_____
_____

Inventory Expenses

Date	Cost ($)	Miles Driven

Location
_____

Entered into PC [ ]

Items Purchased

_____
_____
_____
_____
_____
_____

Date	Cost ($)	Miles Driven

Location
_____

Entered into PC [ ]

Items Purchased

_____
_____
_____
_____
_____
_____

Inventory Expenses

Date	Cost ($)	Miles Driven

Location
_____

Items Purchased
_____
_____
_____
_____
_____
_____
_____
_____

Entered into PC ☐

Date	Cost ($)	Miles Driven

Location
_____

Items Purchased
_____
_____
_____
_____
_____
_____
_____
_____

Entered into PC ☐

Inventory Expenses

Date	Cost ($)	Miles Driven

Location
_____

Entered into PC [ ]

Items Purchased
_____
_____
_____
_____
_____
_____
_____

Date	Cost ($)	Miles Driven

Location
_____

Entered into PC [ ]

Items Purchased
_____
_____
_____
_____
_____
_____
_____

Inventory Expenses

Date	Cost ($)	Miles Driven

Location _____ Entered into PC ☐

Items Purchased

_____
_____
_____
_____
_____
_____
_____

Date	Cost ($)	Miles Driven

Location _____ Entered into PC ☐

Items Purchased

_____
_____
_____
_____
_____
_____
_____

Inventory Expenses

Date	Cost ($)	Miles Driven

Location
_____

Entered into PC [ ]

Items Purchased
_____
_____
_____
_____
_____
_____
_____

Date	Cost ($)	Miles Driven

Location
_____

Entered into PC [ ]

Items Purchased
_____
_____
_____
_____
_____
_____
_____

Inventory Expenses

Date	Cost ($)	Miles Driven

Location _____

Entered into PC [ ]

Items Purchased

_____
_____
_____
_____
_____
_____
_____
_____

Date	Cost ($)	Miles Driven

Location _____

Entered into PC [ ]

Items Purchased

_____
_____
_____
_____
_____
_____
_____
_____

Inventory Expenses

Date	Cost ($)	Miles Driven

Location

_____

Entered into PC ☐

Items Purchased

_____
_____
_____
_____
_____
_____
_____

Date	Cost ($)	Miles Driven

Location

_____

Entered into PC ☐

Items Purchased

_____
_____
_____
_____
_____
_____
_____

Inventory Expenses

Date	Cost ($)	Miles Driven

Location _____   Entered into PC [ ]

Items Purchased

_____

_____

_____

_____

_____

_____

_____

Date	Cost ($)	Miles Driven

Location _____   Entered into PC [ ]

Items Purchased

_____

_____

_____

_____

_____

_____

_____

Inventory Expenses

Date	Cost ($)	Miles Driven

Location
_____   Entered into PC ☐

Items Purchased
_____
_____
_____
_____
_____
_____
_____

Date	Cost ($)	Miles Driven

Location
_____   Entered into PC ☐

Items Purchased
_____
_____
_____
_____
_____
_____
_____

Inventory Expenses

Date	Cost ($)	Miles Driven

Location _____

Entered into PC ☐

Items Purchased

_____
_____
_____
_____
_____
_____
_____

Date	Cost ($)	Miles Driven

Location _____

Entered into PC ☐

Items Purchased

_____
_____
_____
_____
_____
_____
_____

Inventory Expenses

Date	Cost ($)	Miles Driven

Location
_____

Entered into PC [ ]

Items Purchased
_____
_____
_____
_____
_____
_____
_____
_____

Date	Cost ($)	Miles Driven

Location
_____

Entered into PC [ ]

Items Purchased
_____
_____
_____
_____
_____
_____
_____
_____

Inventory Expenses

Date	Cost ($)	Miles Driven

Location _____ Entered into PC ☐

Items Purchased

_____
_____
_____
_____
_____
_____
_____

Date	Cost ($)	Miles Driven

Location _____ Entered into PC ☐

Items Purchased

_____
_____
_____
_____
_____
_____
_____

Inventory Expenses

Date	Cost ($)	Miles Driven

Location
_____

Entered into PC ☐

Items Purchased

_____
_____
_____
_____
_____
_____
_____

Date	Cost ($)	Miles Driven

Location
_____

Entered into PC ☐

Items Purchased

_____
_____
_____
_____
_____
_____
_____

Inventory Expenses

Date	Cost ($)	Miles Driven

Location
_____

Entered into PC [ ]

Items Purchased

_____
_____
_____
_____
_____
_____
_____

Date	Cost ($)	Miles Driven

Location
_____

Entered into PC [ ]

Items Purchased

_____
_____
_____
_____
_____
_____
_____

Inventory Expenses

Date	Cost ($)	Miles Driven

Location
_____

Entered into PC ☐

Items Purchased

_____
_____
_____
_____
_____
_____
_____

Date	Cost ($)	Miles Driven

Location
_____

Entered into PC ☐

Items Purchased

_____
_____
_____
_____
_____
_____
_____

Inventory Expenses

Date	Cost ($)	Miles Driven

Location _____ Entered into PC [ ]

Items Purchased

_____
_____
_____
_____
_____
_____
_____

Date	Cost ($)	Miles Driven

Location _____ Entered into PC [ ]

Items Purchased

_____
_____
_____
_____
_____
_____
_____

Inventory Expenses

Date	Cost ($)	Miles Driven

Location _____ Entered into PC ☐

Items Purchased

_____

_____

_____

_____

_____

_____

_____

Date	Cost ($)	Miles Driven

Location _____ Entered into PC ☐

Items Purchased

_____

_____

_____

_____

_____

_____

_____

Inventory Expenses

Date	Cost ($)	Miles Driven

Location _____

Entered into PC ☐

Items Purchased

_____
_____
_____
_____
_____
_____
_____

Date	Cost ($)	Miles Driven

Location _____

Entered into PC ☐

Items Purchased

_____
_____
_____
_____
_____
_____
_____

Inventory Expenses

Date	Cost ($)	Miles Driven

Location
_____

Entered into PC ☐

Items Purchased

_____
_____
_____
_____
_____
_____

Date	Cost ($)	Miles Driven

Location
_____

Entered into PC ☐

Items Purchased

_____
_____
_____
_____
_____
_____

Inventory Expenses

Date	Cost ($)	Miles Driven

Location _____   Entered into PC ☐

Items Purchased

_____
_____
_____
_____
_____
_____
_____

Date	Cost ($)	Miles Driven

Location _____   Entered into PC ☐

Items Purchased

_____
_____
_____
_____
_____
_____
_____

Inventory Expenses

Date	Cost ($)	Miles Driven

Location _____

Entered into PC ☐

Items Purchased

_____
_____
_____
_____
_____
_____

Date	Cost ($)	Miles Driven

Location _____

Entered into PC ☐

Items Purchased

_____
_____
_____
_____
_____
_____

Inventory Expenses

Date	Cost ($)	Miles Driven

Location
_____

Items Purchased
_____
_____
_____
_____
_____
_____
_____

Entered into PC ☐

Date	Cost ($)	Miles Driven

Location
_____

Items Purchased
_____
_____
_____
_____
_____
_____
_____

Entered into PC ☐

Inventory Expenses

Date	Cost ($)	Miles Driven

Location
_____

Entered into PC ☐

Items Purchased

_____
_____
_____
_____
_____
_____
_____

Date	Cost ($)	Miles Driven

Location
_____

Entered into PC ☐

Items Purchased

_____
_____
_____
_____
_____
_____
_____

Inventory Expenses

Date	Cost ($)	Miles Driven

Location

_____

Entered into PC [ ]

Items Purchased

_____
_____
_____
_____
_____
_____
_____

Date	Cost ($)	Miles Driven

Location

_____

Entered into PC [ ]

Items Purchased

_____
_____
_____
_____
_____
_____
_____

Inventory Expenses

Date	Cost ($)	Miles Driven

Location
_____

Entered into PC [ ]

Items Purchased

_____
_____
_____
_____
_____
_____

Date	Cost ($)	Miles Driven

Location
_____

Entered into PC [ ]

Items Purchased

_____
_____
_____
_____
_____
_____

Inventory Expenses

Date	Cost ($)	Miles Driven

Location _____ Entered into PC [ ]

Items Purchased

_____
_____
_____
_____
_____
_____
_____

Date	Cost ($)	Miles Driven

Location _____ Entered into PC [ ]

Items Purchased

_____
_____
_____
_____
_____
_____
_____

Inventory Expenses

Date	Cost ($)	Miles Driven

Location _____   Entered into PC [ ]

Items Purchased

_____
_____
_____
_____
_____
_____
_____

Date	Cost ($)	Miles Driven

Location _____   Entered into PC [ ]

Items Purchased

_____
_____
_____
_____
_____
_____
_____

Inventory Expenses

Date	Cost ($)	Miles Driven

Location

_____

Items Purchased

Entered into PC ☐

_____
_____
_____
_____
_____
_____
_____

Date	Cost ($)	Miles Driven

Location

_____

Items Purchased

Entered into PC ☐

_____
_____
_____
_____
_____
_____
_____

Inventory Expenses

Date	Cost ($)	Miles Driven

Location
_____

Entered into PC [ ]

Items Purchased

_____
_____
_____
_____
_____
_____

Date	Cost ($)	Miles Driven

Location
_____

Entered into PC [ ]

Items Purchased

_____
_____
_____
_____
_____
_____

Inventory Expenses

Date	Cost ($)	Miles Driven

Location _____ Entered into PC [ ]

Items Purchased

_____
_____
_____
_____
_____
_____
_____

Date	Cost ($)	Miles Driven

Location _____ Entered into PC [ ]

Items Purchased

_____
_____
_____
_____
_____
_____
_____

Inventory Expenses

Date	Cost ($)	Miles Driven

Location
_____

Entered into PC [ ]

Items Purchased

_____
_____
_____
_____
_____
_____

Date	Cost ($)	Miles Driven

Location
_____

Entered into PC [ ]

Items Purchased

_____
_____
_____
_____
_____
_____

Inventory Expenses

Date	Cost ($)	Miles Driven

Location _____ Entered into PC ☐

Items Purchased

_____
_____
_____
_____
_____
_____
_____

Date	Cost ($)	Miles Driven

Location _____ Entered into PC ☐

Items Purchased

_____
_____
_____
_____
_____
_____
_____

Inventory Expenses

Date	Cost ($)	Miles Driven

Location
_____

Entered into PC [ ]

Items Purchased
_____
_____
_____
_____
_____
_____
_____

Date	Cost ($)	Miles Driven

Location
_____

Entered into PC [ ]

Items Purchased
_____
_____
_____
_____
_____
_____
_____

Inventory Expenses

Date	Cost ($)	Miles Driven

Location _____ Entered into PC [ ]

Items Purchased

_____

_____

_____

_____

_____

_____

_____

Date	Cost ($)	Miles Driven

Location _____ Entered into PC [ ]

Items Purchased

_____

_____

_____

_____

_____

_____

_____

Inventory Expenses

Date	Cost ($)	Miles Driven

Location
_____

Entered into PC ☐

Items Purchased
_____
_____
_____
_____
_____
_____
_____

Date	Cost ($)	Miles Driven

Location
_____

Entered into PC ☐

Items Purchased
_____
_____
_____
_____
_____
_____
_____

Inventory Expenses

Date	Cost ($)	Miles Driven

Location _____

Entered into PC ☐

Items Purchased

_____
_____
_____
_____
_____
_____
_____

Date	Cost ($)	Miles Driven

Location _____

Entered into PC ☐

Items Purchased

_____
_____
_____
_____
_____
_____
_____

Inventory Expenses

Date	Cost ($)	Miles Driven

Location
_____

Entered into PC ☐

Items Purchased
_____
_____
_____
_____
_____
_____
_____

Date	Cost ($)	Miles Driven

Location
_____

Entered into PC ☐

Items Purchased
_____
_____
_____
_____
_____
_____
_____

Inventory Expenses

Date	Cost ($)	Miles Driven

Location
_____

Entered into PC ☐

Items Purchased

_____
_____
_____
_____
_____
_____
_____

Date	Cost ($)	Miles Driven

Location
_____

Entered into PC ☐

Items Purchased

_____
_____
_____
_____
_____
_____
_____

Inventory Expenses

Date	Cost ($)	Miles Driven

Location _____   Entered into PC ☐

Items Purchased

_____

_____

_____

_____

_____

_____

Date	Cost ($)	Miles Driven

Location _____   Entered into PC ☐

Items Purchased

_____

_____

_____

_____

_____

_____

Inventory Expenses

Date	Cost ($)	Miles Driven

Location _____ Entered into PC ☐

Items Purchased

_____
_____
_____
_____
_____
_____
_____

Date	Cost ($)	Miles Driven

Location _____ Entered into PC ☐

Items Purchased

_____
_____
_____
_____
_____
_____
_____

Inventory Expenses

Date	Cost ($)	Miles Driven

Location _____ Entered into PC ☐

Items Purchased

_____
_____
_____
_____
_____
_____
_____

Date	Cost ($)	Miles Driven

Location _____ Entered into PC ☐

Items Purchased

_____
_____
_____
_____
_____
_____
_____

Inventory Expenses

Date	Cost ($)	Miles Driven

Location _____

Entered into PC [ ]

Items Purchased

_____
_____
_____
_____
_____
_____
_____

Date	Cost ($)	Miles Driven

Location _____

Entered into PC [ ]

Items Purchased

_____
_____
_____
_____
_____
_____
_____

Inventory Expenses

Date	Cost ($)	Miles Driven

Location
_____

Entered into PC [ ]

Items Purchased
_____
_____
_____
_____
_____
_____

Date	Cost ($)	Miles Driven

Location
_____

Entered into PC [ ]

Items Purchased
_____
_____
_____
_____
_____
_____

Inventory Expenses

Date	Cost ($)	Miles Driven

Location
_____

Entered into PC [ ]

Items Purchased
_____
_____
_____
_____
_____
_____
_____

Date	Cost ($)	Miles Driven

Location
_____

Entered into PC [ ]

Items Purchased
_____
_____
_____
_____
_____
_____
_____

Inventory Expenses

Date	Cost ($)	Miles Driven

Location _____

Entered into PC [ ]

Items Purchased
_____
_____
_____
_____
_____
_____

Date	Cost ($)	Miles Driven

Location _____

Entered into PC [ ]

Items Purchased
_____
_____
_____
_____
_____
_____

Inventory Expenses

Date	Cost ($)	Miles Driven

Location _____ Entered into PC [ ]

Items Purchased

_____
_____
_____
_____
_____
_____
_____

Date	Cost ($)	Miles Driven

Location _____ Entered into PC [ ]

Items Purchased

_____
_____
_____
_____
_____
_____
_____

Inventory Expenses

Date	Cost ($)	Miles Driven

Location _____ Entered into PC [ ]

Items Purchased
_____
_____
_____
_____
_____
_____

Date	Cost ($)	Miles Driven

Location _____ Entered into PC [ ]

Items Purchased
_____
_____
_____
_____
_____
_____

Inventory Expenses

Date	Cost ($)	Miles Driven

Location
_____

Items Purchased

Entered into PC ☐

_____
_____
_____
_____
_____
_____
_____

Date	Cost ($)	Miles Driven

Location
_____

Items Purchased

Entered into PC ☐

_____
_____
_____
_____
_____
_____
_____

Inventory Expenses

Date	Cost ($)	Miles Driven

Location
_____

Entered into PC ☐

Items Purchased

_____
_____
_____
_____
_____
_____

Date	Cost ($)	Miles Driven

Location
_____

Entered into PC ☐

Items Purchased

_____
_____
_____
_____
_____
_____

Inventory Expenses

Date	Cost ($)	Miles Driven

Location _____

Entered into PC ☐

Items Purchased

_____
_____
_____
_____
_____
_____
_____

Date	Cost ($)	Miles Driven

Location _____

Entered into PC ☐

Items Purchased

_____
_____
_____
_____
_____
_____
_____

Inventory Expenses

Date	Cost ($)	Miles Driven

Location

Entered into PC [ ]

_____

Items Purchased

_____
_____
_____
_____
_____
_____

Date	Cost ($)	Miles Driven

Location

Entered into PC [ ]

_____

Items Purchased

_____
_____
_____
_____
_____
_____

Inventory Expenses

Date	Cost ($)	Miles Driven

Location _____ Entered into PC [ ]

Items Purchased

_____
_____
_____
_____
_____
_____
_____

Date	Cost ($)	Miles Driven

Location _____ Entered into PC [ ]

Items Purchased

_____
_____
_____
_____
_____
_____
_____

Inventory Expenses

Date	Cost ($)	Miles Driven

Location _____ Entered into PC ☐

Items Purchased

_____
_____
_____
_____
_____
_____
_____

Date	Cost ($)	Miles Driven

Location _____ Entered into PC ☐

Items Purchased

_____
_____
_____
_____
_____
_____
_____

Inventory Expenses

Date	Cost ($)	Miles Driven

Location _____ Entered into PC [ ]

Items Purchased
_____
_____
_____
_____
_____
_____
_____

Date	Cost ($)	Miles Driven

Location _____ Entered into PC [ ]

Items Purchased
_____
_____
_____
_____
_____
_____
_____

Inventory Expenses

Date	Cost ($)	Miles Driven

Location
_____

Entered into PC [ ]

Items Purchased
_____
_____
_____
_____
_____
_____
_____

Date	Cost ($)	Miles Driven

Location
_____

Entered into PC [ ]

Items Purchased
_____
_____
_____
_____
_____
_____
_____

Inventory Expenses

Date	Cost ($)	Miles Driven

Location
_____

Entered into PC [ ]

Items Purchased
_____
_____
_____
_____
_____
_____
_____
_____

Date	Cost ($)	Miles Driven

Location
_____

Entered into PC [ ]

Items Purchased
_____
_____
_____
_____
_____
_____
_____
_____

Inventory Expenses

Date	Cost ($)	Miles Driven

Location
_____

Entered into PC [ ]

Items Purchased
_____
_____
_____
_____
_____
_____
_____

Date	Cost ($)	Miles Driven

Location
_____

Entered into PC [ ]

Items Purchased
_____
_____
_____
_____
_____
_____
_____

Inventory Expenses

Date	Cost ($)	Miles Driven

Location
_____

Entered into PC ☐

Items Purchased
_____
_____
_____
_____
_____
_____
_____
_____

Date	Cost ($)	Miles Driven

Location
_____

Entered into PC ☐

Items Purchased
_____
_____
_____
_____
_____
_____
_____
_____

Inventory Expenses

Date	Cost ($)	Miles Driven

Location _____

Entered into PC [ ]

Items Purchased

_____

_____

_____

_____

_____

_____

_____

Date	Cost ($)	Miles Driven

Location _____

Entered into PC [ ]

Items Purchased

_____

_____

_____

_____

_____

_____

_____

Inventory Expenses

Date	Cost ($)	Miles Driven

Location
_____

Entered into PC ☐

Items Purchased
_____
_____
_____
_____
_____
_____
_____
_____

Date	Cost ($)	Miles Driven

Location
_____

Entered into PC ☐

Items Purchased
_____
_____
_____
_____
_____
_____
_____
_____

Inventory Expenses

Date	Cost ($)	Miles Driven

Location _____

Entered into PC [ ]

Items Purchased

_____
_____
_____
_____
_____
_____
_____

Date	Cost ($)	Miles Driven

Location _____

Entered into PC [ ]

Items Purchased

_____
_____
_____
_____
_____
_____
_____

Inventory Expenses

Date	Cost ($)	Miles Driven

Location _____ Entered into PC [ ]

Items Purchased

_____
_____
_____
_____
_____
_____
_____

Date	Cost ($)	Miles Driven

Location _____ Entered into PC [ ]

Items Purchased

_____
_____
_____
_____
_____
_____
_____

Inventory Expenses

Date	Cost ($)	Miles Driven

Location
_____

Entered into PC ☐

Items Purchased
_____
_____
_____
_____
_____
_____
_____

Date	Cost ($)	Miles Driven

Location
_____

Entered into PC ☐

Items Purchased
_____
_____
_____
_____
_____
_____
_____

Inventory Expenses

Date	Cost ($)	Miles Driven

Location
_____

Entered into PC [ ]

Items Purchased

_____
_____
_____
_____
_____
_____
_____

Date	Cost ($)	Miles Driven

Location
_____

Entered into PC [ ]

Items Purchased

_____
_____
_____
_____
_____
_____
_____

Inventory Expenses

Date	Cost ($)	Miles Driven

Location _____

Entered into PC ☐

Items Purchased

_____

_____

_____

_____

_____

_____

_____

Date	Cost ($)	Miles Driven

Location _____

Entered into PC ☐

Items Purchased

_____

_____

_____

_____

_____

_____

_____

Inventory Expenses

Date	Cost ($)	Miles Driven

Location
_____

Entered into PC [ ]

Items Purchased
_____
_____
_____
_____
_____
_____
_____

Date	Cost ($)	Miles Driven

Location
_____

Entered into PC [ ]

Items Purchased
_____
_____
_____
_____
_____
_____
_____

Inventory Expenses

Date	Cost ($)	Miles Driven

Location _____

Entered into PC [ ]

Items Purchased

_____
_____
_____
_____
_____
_____
_____

Date	Cost ($)	Miles Driven

Location _____

Entered into PC [ ]

Items Purchased

_____
_____
_____
_____
_____
_____
_____

Inventory Expenses

Date	Cost ($)	Miles Driven

Location
_____

Entered into PC [ ]

Items Purchased
_____
_____
_____
_____
_____
_____
_____

Date	Cost ($)	Miles Driven

Location
_____

Entered into PC [ ]

Items Purchased
_____
_____
_____
_____
_____
_____
_____

Inventory Expenses

Date	Cost ($)	Miles Driven

Location
_____

Entered into PC ☐

Items Purchased
_____
_____
_____
_____
_____
_____
_____

Date	Cost ($)	Miles Driven

Location
_____

Entered into PC ☐

Items Purchased
_____
_____
_____
_____
_____
_____
_____

Inventory Expenses

Date	Cost ($)	Miles Driven

Location _____

Entered into PC [ ]

Items Purchased

_____
_____
_____
_____
_____
_____
_____

Date	Cost ($)	Miles Driven

Location _____

Entered into PC [ ]

Items Purchased

_____
_____
_____
_____
_____
_____
_____

Inventory Expenses

Date	Cost ($)	Miles Driven

Location
_____

Items Purchased
_____
_____
_____
_____
_____
_____

Entered into PC ☐

Date	Cost ($)	Miles Driven

Location
_____

Items Purchased
_____
_____
_____
_____
_____
_____

Entered into PC ☐

Inventory Expenses

Date	Cost ($)	Miles Driven

Location
_____

Entered into PC ☐

Items Purchased

_____
_____
_____
_____
_____
_____
_____
_____

Date	Cost ($)	Miles Driven

Location
_____

Entered into PC ☐

Items Purchased

_____
_____
_____
_____
_____
_____
_____
_____

Inventory Expenses

Date	Cost ($)	Miles Driven

Location
_____

Entered into PC ☐

Items Purchased

_____
_____
_____
_____
_____
_____

Date	Cost ($)	Miles Driven

Location
_____

Entered into PC ☐

Items Purchased

_____
_____
_____
_____
_____
_____

Inventory Expenses

Date	Cost ($)	Miles Driven

Location
_____

Entered into PC [ ]

Items Purchased
_____
_____
_____
_____
_____
_____
_____
_____

Date	Cost ($)	Miles Driven

Location
_____

Entered into PC [ ]

Items Purchased
_____
_____
_____
_____
_____
_____
_____
_____

Inventory Expenses

Date	Cost ($)	Miles Driven

Location
_____

Entered into PC ☐

Items Purchased
_____
_____
_____
_____
_____
_____
_____

Date	Cost ($)	Miles Driven

Location
_____

Entered into PC ☐

Items Purchased
_____
_____
_____
_____
_____
_____
_____

Inventory Expenses

Date	Cost ($)	Miles Driven

Location _____ Entered into PC ☐

Items Purchased

_____
_____
_____
_____
_____
_____
_____

Date	Cost ($)	Miles Driven

Location _____ Entered into PC ☐

Items Purchased

_____
_____
_____
_____
_____
_____
_____

Inventory Expenses

Date	Cost ($)	Miles Driven

Location _____ Entered into PC [ ]

Items Purchased

_____
_____
_____
_____
_____
_____
_____

Date	Cost ($)	Miles Driven

Location _____ Entered into PC [ ]

Items Purchased

_____
_____
_____
_____
_____
_____
_____

Inventory Expenses

Date	Cost ($)	Miles Driven

Location

_____

Entered into PC [ ]

Items Purchased

_____
_____
_____
_____
_____
_____
_____

Date	Cost ($)	Miles Driven

Location

_____

Entered into PC [ ]

Items Purchased

_____
_____
_____
_____
_____
_____
_____

Inventory Expenses

Date	Cost ($)	Miles Driven

Location
_____

Entered into PC [ ]

Items Purchased

_____
_____
_____
_____
_____
_____
_____

Date	Cost ($)	Miles Driven

Location
_____

Entered into PC [ ]

Items Purchased

_____
_____
_____
_____
_____
_____
_____

Inventory Expenses

Date	Cost ($)	Miles Driven

Location _____   Entered into PC [ ]

Items Purchased

_____
_____
_____
_____
_____
_____
_____

Date	Cost ($)	Miles Driven

Location _____   Entered into PC [ ]

Items Purchased

_____
_____
_____
_____
_____
_____
_____

Inventory Expenses

Date	Cost ($)	Miles Driven

Location
_____

Items Purchased
_____
_____
_____
_____
_____
_____
_____

Entered into PC [ ]

Date	Cost ($)	Miles Driven

Location
_____

Items Purchased
_____
_____
_____
_____
_____
_____
_____

Entered into PC [ ]

Inventory Expenses

Date	Cost ($)	Miles Driven

Location _____

Entered into PC ☐

Items Purchased

_____
_____
_____
_____
_____
_____
_____

Date	Cost ($)	Miles Driven

Location _____

Entered into PC ☐

Items Purchased

_____
_____
_____
_____
_____
_____
_____

Inventory Expenses

Date	Cost ($)	Miles Driven

Location _____ Entered into PC [ ]

Items Purchased
_____
_____
_____
_____
_____
_____
_____

Date	Cost ($)	Miles Driven

Location _____ Entered into PC [ ]

Items Purchased
_____
_____
_____
_____
_____
_____
_____

Inventory Expenses

Date	Cost ($)	Miles Driven

Location
_____

Entered into PC [ ]

Items Purchased
_____
_____
_____
_____
_____
_____
_____

Date	Cost ($)	Miles Driven

Location
_____

Entered into PC [ ]

Items Purchased
_____
_____
_____
_____
_____
_____
_____

Inventory Expenses

Date	Cost ($)	Miles Driven

Location
_____

Items Purchased
_____
_____
_____
_____
_____
_____

Entered into PC ☐

Date	Cost ($)	Miles Driven

Location
_____

Items Purchased
_____
_____
_____
_____
_____
_____

Entered into PC ☐

Inventory Expenses

Date	Cost ($)	Miles Driven

Location _____

Entered into PC ☐

Items Purchased

_____
_____
_____
_____
_____
_____
_____

Date	Cost ($)	Miles Driven

Location _____

Entered into PC ☐

Items Purchased

_____
_____
_____
_____
_____
_____
_____

Inventory Expenses

Date	Cost ($)	Miles Driven

Location _____

Entered into PC [ ]

Items Purchased

_____

_____

_____

_____

_____

_____

_____

Date	Cost ($)	Miles Driven

Location _____

Entered into PC [ ]

Items Purchased

_____

_____

_____

_____

_____

_____

_____

Inventory Expenses

Date	Cost ($)	Miles Driven

Location

_____

Entered into PC ☐

Items Purchased

_____
_____
_____
_____
_____
_____
_____

Date	Cost ($)	Miles Driven

Location

_____

Entered into PC ☐

Items Purchased

_____
_____
_____
_____
_____
_____
_____

Inventory Expenses

Date	Cost ($)	Miles Driven

Location _____   Entered into PC [ ]

Items Purchased

_____

_____

_____

_____

_____

_____

_____

Date	Cost ($)	Miles Driven

Location _____   Entered into PC [ ]

Items Purchased

_____

_____

_____

_____

_____

_____

_____

Inventory Expenses

Date	Cost ($)	Miles Driven

Location
_____

Entered into PC [ ]

Items Purchased

_____
_____
_____
_____
_____
_____
_____
_____

Date	Cost ($)	Miles Driven

Location
_____

Entered into PC [ ]

Items Purchased

_____
_____
_____
_____
_____
_____
_____
_____

Inventory Expenses

Date	Cost ($)	Miles Driven

Location

_____ Entered into PC [ ]

Items Purchased

_____
_____
_____
_____
_____
_____
_____

Date	Cost ($)	Miles Driven

Location

_____ Entered into PC [ ]

Items Purchased

_____
_____
_____
_____
_____
_____
_____

Inventory Expenses

Date	Cost ($)	Miles Driven

Location

_____

Entered into PC [ ]

Items Purchased

_____
_____
_____
_____
_____
_____
_____
_____

Date	Cost ($)	Miles Driven

Location

_____

Entered into PC [ ]

Items Purchased

_____
_____
_____
_____
_____
_____
_____
_____

Inventory Expenses

Date	Cost ($)	Miles Driven

Location
_____

Entered into PC ☐

Items Purchased
_____
_____
_____
_____
_____
_____
_____

Date	Cost ($)	Miles Driven

Location
_____

Entered into PC ☐

Items Purchased
_____
_____
_____
_____
_____
_____
_____

Inventory Expenses

Date	Cost ($)	Miles Driven

Location
_____

Entered into PC [ ]

Items Purchased
_____
_____
_____
_____
_____
_____
_____

Date	Cost ($)	Miles Driven

Location
_____

Entered into PC [ ]

Items Purchased
_____
_____
_____
_____
_____
_____
_____

Inventory Expenses

Date	Cost ($)	Miles Driven

Location
_____

Items Purchased

_____
_____
_____
_____
_____
_____
_____

Entered into PC ☐

Date	Cost ($)	Miles Driven

Location
_____

Items Purchased

_____
_____
_____
_____
_____
_____
_____

Entered into PC ☐

Inventory Expenses

Date	Cost ($)	Miles Driven

Location
_____

Items Purchased

_____
_____
_____
_____
_____
_____
_____
_____

Entered into PC ☐

Date	Cost ($)	Miles Driven

Location
_____

Items Purchased

_____
_____
_____
_____
_____
_____
_____
_____

Entered into PC ☐

Inventory Expenses

Date	Cost ($)	Miles Driven

Location

_____   Entered into PC ☐

Items Purchased

_____
_____
_____
_____
_____
_____

Date	Cost ($)	Miles Driven

Location

_____   Entered into PC ☐

Items Purchased

_____
_____
_____
_____
_____
_____

Inventory Expenses

Date	Cost ($)	Miles Driven

Location
_____

Entered into PC [ ]

Items Purchased

_____
_____
_____
_____
_____
_____
_____

Date	Cost ($)	Miles Driven

Location
_____

Entered into PC [ ]

Items Purchased

_____
_____
_____
_____
_____
_____
_____

Inventory Expenses

Date	Cost ($)	Miles Driven

Location _____

Entered into PC ☐

Items Purchased

_____
_____
_____
_____
_____
_____
_____

Date	Cost ($)	Miles Driven

Location _____

Entered into PC ☐

Items Purchased

_____
_____
_____
_____
_____
_____
_____

Inventory Expenses

Date	Cost ($)	Miles Driven

Location _____ Entered into PC ☐

Items Purchased

_____
_____
_____
_____
_____
_____
_____

Date	Cost ($)	Miles Driven

Location _____ Entered into PC ☐

Items Purchased

_____
_____
_____
_____
_____
_____
_____

Inventory Expenses

Date	Cost ($)	Miles Driven

Location _____

Entered into PC ☐

Items Purchased

_____
_____
_____
_____
_____
_____
_____

Date	Cost ($)	Miles Driven

Location _____

Entered into PC ☐

Items Purchased

_____
_____
_____
_____
_____
_____
_____

Inventory Expenses

Date	Cost ($)	Miles Driven

Location _____   Entered into PC ☐

Items Purchased

_____
_____
_____
_____
_____
_____
_____

Date	Cost ($)	Miles Driven

Location _____   Entered into PC ☐

Items Purchased

_____
_____
_____
_____
_____
_____
_____

Inventory Expenses

Date	Cost ($)	Miles Driven

Location _____

Entered into PC ☐

Items Purchased

_____
_____
_____
_____
_____
_____

Date	Cost ($)	Miles Driven

Location _____

Entered into PC ☐

Items Purchased

_____
_____
_____
_____
_____
_____

Inventory Expenses

Date	Cost ($)	Miles Driven

Location
_____

Entered into PC [ ]

Items Purchased

_____
_____
_____
_____
_____
_____
_____

Date	Cost ($)	Miles Driven

Location
_____

Entered into PC [ ]

Items Purchased

_____
_____
_____
_____
_____
_____
_____

Inventory Expenses

Date	Cost ($)	Miles Driven

Location
_____

Entered into PC ☐

Items Purchased
_____
_____
_____
_____
_____
_____
_____

Date	Cost ($)	Miles Driven

Location
_____

Entered into PC ☐

Items Purchased
_____
_____
_____
_____
_____
_____
_____

Inventory Expenses

Date	Cost ($)	Miles Driven

Location _____ Entered into PC ☐

Items Purchased

_____

_____

_____

_____

_____

_____

_____

Date	Cost ($)	Miles Driven

Location _____ Entered into PC ☐

Items Purchased

_____

_____

_____

_____

_____

_____

_____

Inventory Expenses

Date	Cost ($)	Miles Driven

Location
_____

Entered into PC [ ]

Items Purchased
_____
_____
_____
_____
_____
_____
_____

Date	Cost ($)	Miles Driven

Location
_____

Entered into PC [ ]

Items Purchased
_____
_____
_____
_____
_____
_____
_____

Inventory Expenses

Date	Cost ($)	Miles Driven

Location
_____ Entered into PC [ ]

Items Purchased
_____
_____
_____
_____
_____
_____
_____

Date	Cost ($)	Miles Driven

Location
_____ Entered into PC [ ]

Items Purchased
_____
_____
_____
_____
_____
_____
_____

Inventory Expenses

Date	Cost ($)	Miles Driven

Location

_____

Entered into PC ☐

Items Purchased

_____
_____
_____
_____
_____
_____
_____

Date	Cost ($)	Miles Driven

Location

_____

Entered into PC ☐

Items Purchased

_____
_____
_____
_____
_____
_____
_____

Inventory Expenses

Date	Cost ($)	Miles Driven

Location _____ Entered into PC ☐

Items Purchased

_____
_____
_____
_____
_____
_____
_____

Date	Cost ($)	Miles Driven

Location _____ Entered into PC ☐

Items Purchased

_____
_____
_____
_____
_____
_____
_____

Inventory Expenses

Date	Cost ($)	Miles Driven

Location
_____

Entered into PC [ ]

Items Purchased
_____
_____
_____
_____
_____
_____
_____

Date	Cost ($)	Miles Driven

Location
_____

Entered into PC [ ]

Items Purchased
_____
_____
_____
_____
_____
_____
_____

Inventory Expenses

Date	Cost ($)	Miles Driven

Location _____ Entered into PC ☐

Items Purchased

_____
_____
_____
_____
_____
_____
_____

Date	Cost ($)	Miles Driven

Location _____ Entered into PC ☐

Items Purchased

_____
_____
_____
_____
_____
_____
_____

Inventory Expenses

Date	Cost ($)	Miles Driven

Location _____

Entered into PC [ ]

Items Purchased

_____
_____
_____
_____
_____
_____
_____

Date	Cost ($)	Miles Driven

Location _____

Entered into PC [ ]

Items Purchased

_____
_____
_____
_____
_____
_____
_____

Inventory Expenses

Date	Cost ($)	Miles Driven

Location _____ Entered into PC ☐

Items Purchased

_____
_____
_____
_____
_____
_____
_____

Date	Cost ($)	Miles Driven

Location _____ Entered into PC ☐

Items Purchased

_____
_____
_____
_____
_____
_____
_____

Inventory Expenses

Date	Cost ($)	Miles Driven

Location
_____

Entered into PC ☐

Items Purchased
_____
_____
_____
_____
_____
_____
_____

Date	Cost ($)	Miles Driven

Location
_____

Entered into PC ☐

Items Purchased
_____
_____
_____
_____
_____
_____
_____

Inventory Expenses

Date	Cost ($)	Miles Driven

Location   Entered into PC ☐
_____

Items Purchased

_____
_____
_____
_____
_____
_____
_____

Date	Cost ($)	Miles Driven

Location   Entered into PC ☐
_____

Items Purchased

_____
_____
_____
_____
_____
_____
_____

Inventory Expenses

Date	Cost ($)	Miles Driven

Location _____

Entered into PC ☐

Items Purchased
_____
_____
_____
_____
_____
_____
_____

Date	Cost ($)	Miles Driven

Location _____

Entered into PC ☐

Items Purchased
_____
_____
_____
_____
_____
_____
_____

Inventory Expenses

Date	Cost ($)	Miles Driven

Location _____ Entered into PC ☐

Items Purchased

_____
_____
_____
_____
_____
_____
_____
_____

Date	Cost ($)	Miles Driven

Location _____ Entered into PC ☐

Items Purchased

_____
_____
_____
_____
_____
_____
_____
_____

Inventory Expenses

Date	Cost ($)	Miles Driven

Location _____ Entered into PC ☐

Items Purchased

_____
_____
_____
_____
_____
_____
_____

Date	Cost ($)	Miles Driven

Location _____ Entered into PC ☐

Items Purchased

_____
_____
_____
_____
_____
_____
_____

Inventory Expenses

Date	Cost ($)	Miles Driven

Location
_____

Entered into PC [ ]

Items Purchased

_____
_____
_____
_____
_____
_____
_____

Date	Cost ($)	Miles Driven

Location
_____

Entered into PC [ ]

Items Purchased

_____
_____
_____
_____
_____
_____
_____

Inventory Expenses

Date	Cost ($)	Miles Driven

Location
_____

Entered into PC [ ]

Items Purchased

_____
_____
_____
_____
_____
_____
_____

Date	Cost ($)	Miles Driven

Location
_____

Entered into PC [ ]

Items Purchased

_____
_____
_____
_____
_____
_____
_____

Inventory Expenses

Date	Cost ($)	Miles Driven

Location
_____

Entered into PC [ ]

Items Purchased
_____
_____
_____
_____
_____
_____
_____

Date	Cost ($)	Miles Driven

Location
_____

Entered into PC [ ]

Items Purchased
_____
_____
_____
_____
_____
_____
_____

Inventory Expenses

Date	Cost ($)	Miles Driven

Location
_____

Items Purchased   Entered into PC [ ]

_____
_____
_____
_____
_____
_____
_____

Date	Cost ($)	Miles Driven

Location
_____

Items Purchased   Entered into PC [ ]

_____
_____
_____
_____
_____
_____
_____

Inventory Expenses

Date	Cost ($)	Miles Driven

Location
_____

Items Purchased
_____
_____
_____
_____
_____
_____
_____

Entered into PC ☐

Date	Cost ($)	Miles Driven

Location
_____

Items Purchased
_____
_____
_____
_____
_____
_____
_____

Entered into PC ☐

Inventory Expenses

Date	Cost ($)	Miles Driven

Location

_____

Entered into PC [ ]

Items Purchased

_____
_____
_____
_____
_____
_____
_____

Date	Cost ($)	Miles Driven

Location

_____

Entered into PC [ ]

Items Purchased

_____
_____
_____
_____
_____
_____
_____

Inventory Expenses

Date	Cost ($)	Miles Driven

Location _____   Entered into PC ☐

Items Purchased

_____
_____
_____
_____
_____
_____

Date	Cost ($)	Miles Driven

Location _____   Entered into PC ☐

Items Purchased

_____
_____
_____
_____
_____
_____

www.ingramcontent.com/pod-product-compliance
Lightning Source LLC
Chambersburg PA
CBHW072140170526
45158CB00004BA/1448